MW00966315

the māori world

photography by margaret kawharu, james heremaia and serena stevenson

REED

Reed Publishing (NZ) Ltd
Te Karuhi tā tāpui o Reed (Aotearoa)

Established in 1907, Reed is New Zealand's largest
book publisher, with over 300 titles in print.

For details on all these books visit our website:
www.reed.co.nz

Published by Reed Books, a division of Reed Publishing (NZ) Ltd, 39 Rawene Road, Birkenhead, Auckland 10.
Associated companics, branchcs and representatives throughout the world.

ISBN 0 7900 1021 6
First published 2005

National Library of New Zealand Cataloguing-in-Publication Data

Kawharu, Margaret.
The Māori world : a pictorial record / [Margaret Kawharu, James
Heremaia and Serena Stevenson].
ISBN 0-7900-1021-6
1. Maori (New Zealand people)–Social life and customs–
Pictorial works. I. Heremaia, James. II. Stevenson, Serena.
III. Title.
305.899442–dc 22

Design by Cheryl Rowe

Printed in China

contents

foreword

He aha te mea nui o te ao? What is the most important thing in the world?
He tangata, he tangata, he tangata. It is people, it is people, it is people.

No matter how breathtaking the mountain, or how magnificent the pristine stretch of beach, it is the conversations and moments shared with New Zealanders that make time spent in the country so memorable.

The Maori culture has been indigenous to Aotearoa/New Zealand since its seafaring people (originally from Polynesia) began settling here around the thirteenth century AD, and it still plays an important role in our nation's growth today. Maori beliefs place strong emphasis on the importance of family and community, and living in harmony with nature. They inhabit a unique and spiritual world full of legends and history that enriches the fabric of Aotearoa/New Zealand.

This pictorial record is a window into the everyday world of Maori people. Snapshots of marae life, social customs, taonga (or treasures), important places and employment today illustrate how Maori live in the present while constantly remembering the past and honouring their ancestors.

It also utilises the talents of photographers whose pictures tell Maori stories through their personal understanding of the culture. Their insights help to highlight the importance of Maori alongside other indigenous cultures.

Enjoy this journey into the Maori world.

Tena koutou, tena koutou, tena koutou katoa. Welcome to all.

WAITANGI, 2004

Young men perform the haka, a war dance traditionally used to intimidate enemies before battle. The stamping feet and rousing cries of a haka make it a spine-tingling ritual to experience; the All Blacks rugby team perform one before each game they play.

Dame Whina Cooper was a well-respected elder and Maori rights activist. In 1975, at 80 years old,
she led a 1126 km-march from the far North to Wellington to highlight land rights concerns.

FORESHORE AND SEABED HIKOI, AUCKLAND, 2004

ABOVE: A young girl wraps up against the cold at an outdoor gathering, proudly wearing her pounamu, or greenstone, earrings and pendant.

RIGHT: Whanau, or extended families, often play a large part in bringing up children, especially in rural areas.

A young boy hitches a ride during a demonstration march in Auckland.

The Maori people journeyed to Aotearoa/New Zealand from their ancestral home in Polynesia, navigating the Pacific Ocean through their knowledge of stars and patterns of wind, cloud and currents.

HARA TANGA MARAE, KENNEDY BAY

ABOVE: Lying at the feet of their ancestors — mokopuna, the young generation, sprawl on the floor below carvings representing their forebears.

LEFT: The faces found in wood carvings represent a tribe's whakapapa, or ancestors, and the shape of each head denotes the tribal area from which it comes.

Brandishing a pounamu mere, or short club, this Maori warrior's fierce demeanour and protruding tongue means he's ready for battle.

As with most indigenous cultures, older Maori (such as these two koroua) are respected for their life experience and their knowledge of culture and history.

Two worlds meet at the ground-breaking Ruatoki School, in the Bay of Plenty. In 1978 it became the first school to teach in both English and Maori in a Maori-speaking community.

FORESHORE AND SEABED HIKOI, WELLINGTON, 2004

Protestors march through downtown Wellington to air their concerns outside Parliament, also known as the Beehive.

FORESHORE AND SEABED HIKOI, AUCKLAND HARBOUR BRIDGE, 2004

Demonstrating across the generations for Maori land rights. Disputes over land ownership,
stretching back to the Treaty of Waitangi signing in 1840, are gradually being resolved through a dedicated tribunal.

This rippling flag of black, white and red represents the tino rangatiratanga movement — a group who believe that Maori should be allowed to rule themselves without government intervention.

ABOVE: Foreshore and seabed hikoi supporters on Auckland's waterfront in 2004. In the 1950s and 1960s, many Maori moved from rural to urban areas in search of work, often losing their tribal connections.

RIGHT: Rosy colours wash over Mt Egmont/Taranaki — legend has it this mountain was banished from the central North Island after losing a battle for the affections of beautiful Mt Pihanga.

ABOVE: The whare nui, or meeting house, at Waitangi — on the grounds of this marae in 1840, the Treaty of Waitangi was signed by Maori and Queen Victoria's representatives.

RIGHT: Kaikoura township stands alone on a rocky peninsula, with the beautiful snow-capped Kaikoura mountains in the distance. The remains of several pa, or settlements, from years ago still exist to this day.

ABOVE: Morning mist enshrouds the fields of Northland, a relatively untouched area of the country that has particularly strong spiritual connections for Maori.

RIGHT: Boiling thermal mud at Whakarewarewa, near Rotorua. The town of Rotorua is a tourist destination popular
for the spectacle of its natural hot springs, steam vents and erupting geysers.

Living off and nurturing the land while preserving it for future generations is a central part of the Maori ethos
— the tangata whenua, or people of the land, have a strong spiritual relationship with the natural world.

Sleeping is a communal affair on most marae, which is a focal point of a Maori community. People sleep side-by-side on mattresses in the whare nui.

ABOVE: The interior of this meeting house features a combination of crafts — wood carving, painted drawings, and tukutuku or woven flax panels.

Inside a whare nui, which is designed to reflect the human body. The high ridge running the length of the building is the tahuhu, its spine, while the heke, or sloping carved wooden panels, symbolise the ribs.

A strong contender for the title of 'most beautiful falls in New Zealand', the 30m-high Marokopa Falls are found near Kawhia, on the North Island's east coast.

The whare nui at Auckland Museum, where a cultural group performs daily shows of song, poi dances, stick games, weaponry and the famous haka for visitors and locals alike.

An elder prepares to speak at a gathering. Maori is an oral tradition, so knowledge and legends are commonly passed down by word-of-mouth.

Onlookers are dwarfed by clouds of steam rising from the frequently erupting Pohutu Geyser, in Rotorua's Whakarewarewa thermal reserve.

ABOVE: A group of visitors is welcomed on to a marae by the karanga, or calling, of two women in black, while schoolchildren nearby prepare to sing a waiata, or song.

RIGHT: The hongi is a greeting, where two people press noses (and sometimes foreheads), exchanging the breath of life
— this means the visitors are no longer strangers, but now tangata whenua.

ABOVE TOP: Members of a host tribe perform a passionate haka and song for visitors, watched over by tribal ancestors in the photos behind them.

ABOVE BELOW: Pulling up a hangi — a feast of meat, kumara and other vegetables cooked by heated stones in an enclosed earth oven.

RIGHT: The young are encouraged to join kapa haka groups, enriching their knowledge of Maori culture and cultivating a love of performing.

ABOVE: The deep, mournful sound of the putatara (or conch shell) signals a call to attention during a ceremony or a warning of danger — the bigger the shell, the deeper the sound.

LEFT: Paddlers from a waka, or canoe, get close to the earth before taking to the sea — as their ancestors did over 1000 years ago, travelling in large ocean-going waka that carried them across the Pacific Ocean.

ABOVE: When the native pohutukawa tree blossoms in summer, coastal areas come alight with bright red flowers. Pohutukawa is also known as the native Christmas tree.

RIGHT: Renewed interest in New Zealand's indigenous culture means more people are keen to learn about working in traditional arts.
This work was crafted by a student at a carving school in the Wellington region.

KAI HOE MAHUHU-KI-TE-RANGI

ABOVE: Ta moko designs may look like ordinary tattoos, but traditionally they were finely chiselled into the skin and stained with ink. They symbolise anything from whakapapa to individual and tribal identity, and men and women both wear moko.

RIGHT: Hours of intricate carving work went into this tokotoko, or walking stick, which is now on display at the National Museum in London.

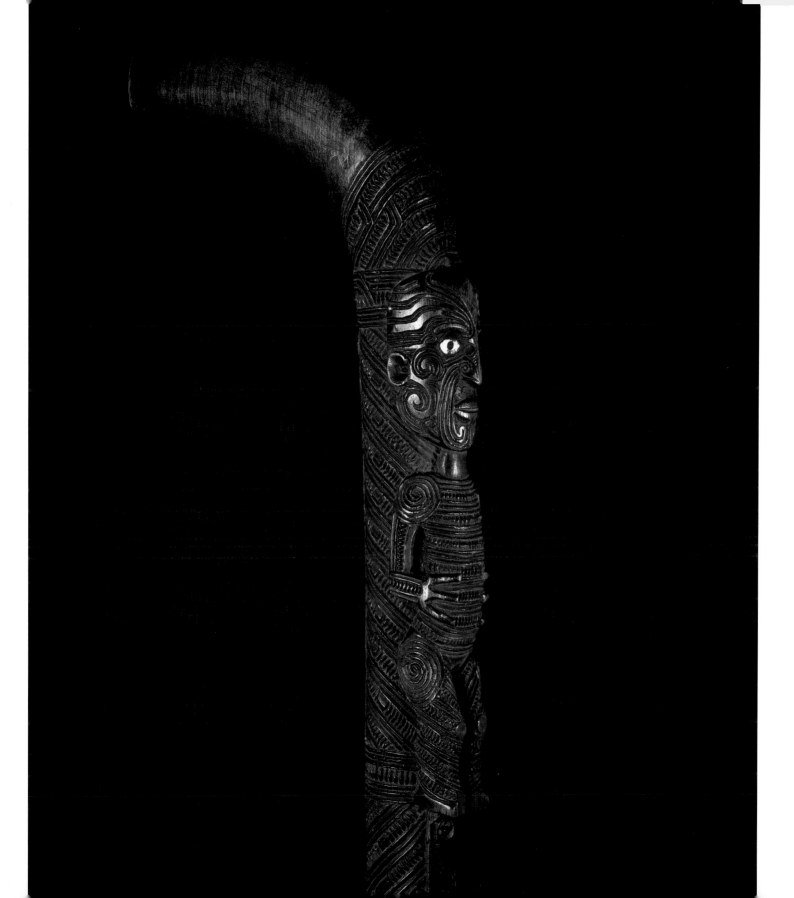

ABOVE LEFT: What looks like an unremarkable piece of pounamu can become a beautiful work of art through patient, delicate carving.

ABOVE RIGHT: Nimble fingers weave fronds of harakeke, or flax, into a small kete, or bag, examples of which are lined up against the wall.

RIGHT: Decorative cloaks, or kakahu, such as this example woven by Erenora Puketapu-Heteta and adorned with kiwi feathers, are highly prized and only worn by chiefs or very respected members of a tribe.

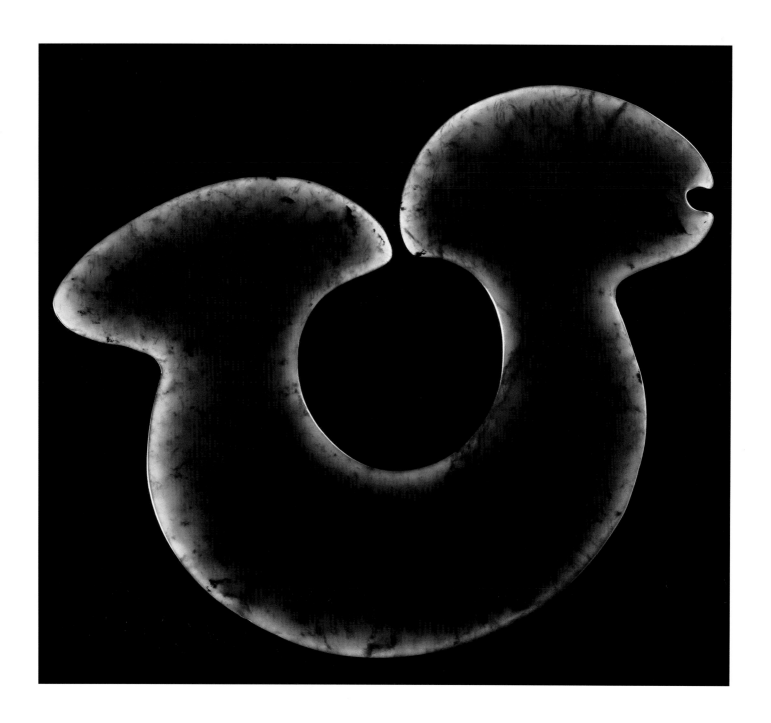

Pounamu is most plentiful on the West Coast of the South Island, and is regarded as a taonga — a treasure that is held dear by Maori.

Wood carvers etch designs into the timber in its natural, uncoloured state. Once the dust and chips are blown away, the carving is painted in the rich red-brown colour common to most marae.

ABOVE: The graceful curling shape of this bone carving is reminiscent of the koru, a spiral motif commonly found in Maori art that represents a fern frond unfurling.

LEFT: A warrior lays down a wero, or challenge, to start the powhiri, or welcoming ceremony. A member of the visiting party must respectfully pick it up to indicate their peaceful intentions.

ABOVE & RIGHT: Although they are often used as a durable, practical bag, kete are becoming decorative works of art in their own right, embellished with feathers, shells and down.

FORESHORE AND SEABED HIKOI, WELLINGTON, 2004

ABOVE: Piupiu, or short skirt, are traditionally made from harakeke or flax, although other materials are sometimes used. The shell-stripped flax leaf is softened before carving and dyeing. As the flax dries, it curls into a cylindrical shape that is woven to a plaited waistband.

LEFT: Preparing to launch inflatable boats for another day of whale watching, an integral part of the tourist industry in Kaikoura. Whales hold special significance in tribal history, as seen in the acclaimed movie Whale Rider.

TE PURU O TAMAKI — TAKAPARAWHAU

ABOVE: Every year, festivals and competitions around the country showcase kapa haka performances. Using the poi (pictured, a soft swinging ball on a plaited rope) requires excellent hand-eye coordination.

RIGHT: Spending time in the sun: a kuia, or elder, reads to two mokopuna in front of a whare nui. Marae are places for community activities and social gatherings, as well as more formal functions.

LEFT: When Tom Cruise came to Taranaki to film *The Last Samurai*, he was greeted by a traditional Maori welcome, including a hongi.

ABOVE: Children line up outside a kohanga reo, a total-immersion pre-school, where Maori is the only language spoken and taught.

ABOVE: The Maori language, at times close to dying out, is gaining strength and popularity once more. Here, a young boy cuts his teeth on a Maori translation of a popular children's book about Spot the dog.

RIGHT: Fishermen check their cages for kai moana, or food of the sea. One of the most famous Maori legends is about a god named Maui who 'fished' up the North Island while on a fishing trip with his brothers.

ABOVE: Packing karengo, or dried seaweed, one of the native ingredients that is riding the trend of renewed interest in indigenous foods. Other popular ingredients are pikopiko, small curly fern fronds similar to asparagus, and horopito, a peppery bush plant.

RIGHT: This kuia has a moko, or facial tattoo that covers both her chin and lips. In more traditional times, full blue lips were regarded as a strong indicator of feminine beauty.

ABOVE TOP: Rugby is a popular game among Maori, from playing recreational games on a Saturday afternoon to supporting the world-class All Blacks.

ABOVE BELOW: Guided by their culture's values and protocols, many Maori are now making their way in the Pakeha-dominated business world.

FORESHORE AND SEABED HIKOI, WELLINGTON, 2004

Fellowship unites Maori in support of their kaupapa. While historical grievances are still being addressed,
Maori are establishing a strong, confident voice in today's society.

glossary

Kia ora.	Greeting, acknowledgement or thank you (literally, 'good health').
Tena koe.	Hello (to one person).
Tena korua.	Hello (to two people).
Tena koutou.	Hello (to three or more people).
Morena.	Good morning.
Kei te pehea koe?	How are you?
Kei te pai ahau!	I'm good!
Kaore i te pai!	I'm not good/not well!
Kia pai.	Be good.
Kia kaha.	Be strong.
Ka kite ano.	See you again.
Haera ra.	Good bye (when the other person is leaving).
E noho ra.	Good bye (when the speaker is leaving).
Hei kona ra.	Good bye (when speaking by telephone).

1	tahi	**7**	whitu
2	rua	**8**	waru
3	toru	**9**	iwa
4	wha	**10**	tekau
5	rima	**11**	tekau ma tahi
6	ono	**20**	rua tekau ...

ae	yes
Aotearoa	New Zealand
aroha	love
haka	war dance
hangi	earth oven cooked feast
hapu	sub-tribe
harakeke	flax
hongi	press noses in greeting
horopito	a peppery bush plant used in cooking
iwi	tribe
kai	food
kai moana	food from the sea
kakahu	cloak
karanga	ceremonial call of welcome
karengo	dried seaweed
kete	basket
koha	donation or expression of thanks
kohanga	nursery
koru	spiral of life unfolding
koro	old man
koroua	old men
kuia	old woman

mana	prestige
Maori	native people
marae	focal point of settlement
mauri	life principle
mere	short club
moko	tattoo
mokopuna	young generation
pa	village
Pakeha	non-Maori people
pikopiko	curled fern used in cooking
poi	a soft swinging ball on a plaited rope
pounamu	greenstone
powhiri	welcoming ceremony
tangata	person (either sex)
tangata whenua	people of the land
taonga	treasure
tapu	sacred
tokotoko	walking stick
waka	canoe
whakapapa	genealogy or ancestors
whanau	extended family
whare nui	meeting house
whare	house

Photo credits Margaret Kawharu – contents page, p.7, 9, 12, 15, 22, 23–26, 28, 29, 31, 38, 41–43, 45–47, 49, 50–52, 54, 57–60.   James Heremaia – front cover, p.11, 14, 21, 34–37, 39, 44, 55, 56.   Serena Stevenson – title page, p.6, 8, 10, 13, 17–20, 27, 32, 53, 63.   All other photos from Reed Publishing (NZ) Ltd.